# Petals
## of Wisdom

# Petals of Wisdom

WRITTEN BY

## PATRICIA MOCK

XULON PRESS

Xulon Press
2301 Lucien Way #415
Maitland, FL 32751
407.339.4217
www.xulonpress.com

Printed in the United States of America.

ISBN-13: 9781545645185

Simply slipping in a puddle
on a cold December day
painfully waiting to be found...
and yet at the very same time
entering a different season of life
and
a Classroom with new lessons to be learned.
This collection of personal,
spiritual Insights
includes glimpses into life
I gleaned while healing from a
fractured back
the following six months ...and counting!

All Scripture references are NIV 1984

Do everything
without
complaining...

Philippians 2:14

If I truly cherish the lessons
I am learning
Then I should embrace them
just as I would a
"Bouquet of Blessings"...
Embrace The process
And
Quit Complaining!

Psalms 119:68; Philippians 2:14-15

...Through Christ
Our comfort
Overflows.


2 Corinthians 1:5

I have learned my sorrow
can become a
**"bridge"**

to another's suffering...

2 Corinthians 1:3-5

... teach me.

Psalm 119:68

Seek Comfort

But desire

God's deepest Truth

Matthew 5:4; Psalm 119:65-68;71

...Make Music in your heart!...

Ephesians 5:19

Don't underestimate
the strength of a simple
melody,
with all its beauty,
to lift the heaviest weight
of a burdened soul

Psalm 59:16-17; Ephesians 5:19

...do not lose heart.

2 Corinthians 4:16

It is often at my
Lowest point

That I discover God's
highest blessings
and
purposes

2 Corinthians 4:16-17

A cheerful heart is good medicine...

Proverbs 17:22

Blessed are those
who care for the weak.

Psalm 41:1

How VERY blessed
are the weak
who are cared for...

CHEERFULLY!

Proverbs 17:22

The Golden Rule...

Matthew 7:12

My good intentions
don't really count much...
except to me!
They certainly don't
help or mean much to others...
unless I act on them!

+ Good Intentions

- Without actions

_____

= 0

Matthew 7:12

The heart ...

weighs its answers...

Proverbs 15:28

"Sift" through your
Feelings carefully...
Before you decide
What to
"bake"
With Them!

Proverbs 15:28; Ephesians 4:2-3; 5:15-17

... light dawns for the upright...

Psalm 112:4

When feeling lost in the
darkness of the forest
remember to look up to the
opening of heaven's light

It's there!

2 Peter 1:19; Psalm 36:9, 112:4

...God disciplines us
for our good.

Hebrews 12:10

Consider any
disappointment
or
adversity
as discipline from the Father's
hand and you will always find
something of great value

Hebrews 12:5-11

Direct my footsteps...

Psalm 119:133

Don't
Miss
The
Road
Sign
When
Life
Takes

a Sudden            turn

Psalm 119:133; Proverbs 3:5-6

... testing of your faith
develops perseverance....

James 1: 3

# SNARES

come from the Father of Lies

to get us off track

Proverbs 3:26; Galatians 5:7


# TRIALS

come from the

Father of Love and Light

with opportunities to


STAY the Course!

James 1:2-4

... the Lord's purpose prevails.

Proverbs 19:21

We sense God's

handprint in

different circumstances...

Imagine if we could see

with physical eyes

His handprints

over the course of a lifetime!

Proverbs 16:9, 19:21

... encourage one another...
Hebrews 10:25

In "times of need"
our needs may vary

But
what we **ALL** need

is to know others care!

Colossians 4:8; Philippians 2:20
Hebrews 10:25

... consider others
better than yourselves.

Philippians 2:3

It's simple math
with profound comfort...

# 1 + 1 =2

when you feel alone,
"simply"
reach out to someone else!

Ephesians 5:1-2; Philippians 2:3

The Lord remembers ...

Psalm 115:12

I May forget others ...
They may forget me...

BUT

God remembers us all

Psalm 115:12 -13

Psalm 139:17

Ask ...

Seek ...

Knock ...

... the door will be opened.

....

Matthew 7:7-8

We should never be dismayed
at how God answers prayer!
No matter what it may seem
or how it might appear,
He only answers in

and

<u>never</u>

with "snakes or stones!"

Matthew 7:7-11

Be filled with the Spirit...

Ephesians 5:18

I may not be able to
create music today
but
I can enjoy harmony
with the
Father,
Son,
and
Holy Spirit

Ephesians 5:18-20; 1 Peter 1:2

Teach us
to number
our days aright ...

Psalm 90:12

MOURN AS I MUST,
BUT TRY NOT TO USE
PRECIOUS TIME
GRIEVING OVER
WHAT CANNOT BE ...

AND SPEND MORE TIME
Moving TOWARD
THAT WHICH CAN!

Psalm 90:12

...look

<u>also</u> to the interests of others.

Philippians 2:4

Somehow I get so wrapped up
In all that concerns
<u>me</u>
That I miss the entanglements
others
are encountering

Philippians 2:3-4

41

... I call this to mind ...

I have hope ...

Lamentations 3:19

It's great that...

God's love and faithfulness

Reaches to the skies!

But it is <u>so</u> amazing as I see it

expressed in the

"4 walls of my

own                     and life!"

Lamentations 3:19-23; Psalm 57:10

...there are many parts,

but one body.

1 Corinthians 12:20

If shoes are not
"one size fits all,"
why would I think others
Could understand what it is
to walk in my
8 ½ narrow sandals?

Colossians 4:7-9; Philippians 1:27

I Corinthians 12:20

Lord,
we rely on You.

2 Chronicles 14:11

Blessings come in a variety of ways...

For only...

when there was no other alternative

I was reminded to

**RELY ON GOD ALONE.**

2 Corinthians 1:8-9; 2 Chronicles 14:11, 20:1-30

O Lord...
listen to my cry.

Psalm 17 :1

A most profound
and humble blessing
is
learning to literally ...

cry out to God

Psalm 10:17, 17:1, 130:1-2

... the Lord turns
my darkness
into light.

2 Samuel 22:29

When fears arise
in the darkness,
God will always
provide the
Light!

Psalm 27:1, 84:11; Isaiah 60:1
2 Samuel 22:29

51

Your love has given me
great joy and encouragement,

Philemon 7

Even the lightest
"shower of blessing"
Can provide the greatest
encouragement
for the soul!


Philemon 7; Proverbs 11:25;

Love is

...patient
...kind
...not self-seeking...

I Corinthians 13:13

"In sickness and in health"

Means

In sickness and in health!

n reality,

It's a beautiful thing to watch!

1 Corinthians 13:1-13

And,

we <u>know</u>

in all things…

Romans 8:28

The only expectation
that doesn't disappoint is
knowing with certainty that
God doesn't disappoint
And
works everything for good
for those who love Him...

Romans 8:28; 1 Peter 4:19

May the God of all hope
fill you with all joy and peace...

Romans 15:13

Blessings....

There is

Joy ... in His presence

Comfort... in His peace

Power ... in His perspective

All He alone can give!

1 Corinthians 2:9-10; Romans 15:13

He heals the brokenhearted ...

Psalm 147:3

Broken bones
take 100 days to heal

Broken hearts
take much longer

1 Peter 5:7; Psalm 147:3

... be quick to listen

James 1:19

I shouldn't ask, "How are you?"
unless ...

I am interested enough
to listen to the answer!

James 1:19

Turn my eyes...
From worthless things;

Psalm 119:37

If I find myself
lacking in my hunger
for God's Word...
Maybe I'm feeding on too much
"junk food!"

Psalm 119:36-37

Search me, O God,

Psalm 139: 23

My mirror
Kindly reflects
my
appearance
but


is <u>not</u> an accurate reflection
...of who I really am


1 Samuel 16:7; Psalm 139:23-24

Be kind and compassionate...

Ephesians 4: 32

This above all: to thine own self

be TRUE.

-William Shakespeare

# TRUTH

<u>Sometimes</u> this translates

Be truthful to others

always in kindness

and Certainly in love

Proverbs 3:3-4; Ephesians 4:15; 32

Put your hope in God...

Psalm 42:11

Depression comes like a
"Flag of Feelings!"
Instead of giving it a full salute,
Counter with a "Flag of Facts"
that might require
action or acceptance
**Waved in faith!**

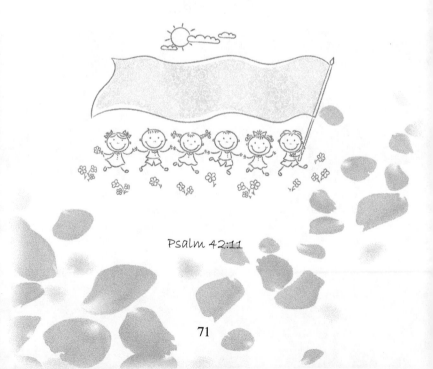

Psalm 42:11

May the words of my mouth ...
be pleasing in your sight
O, Lord...

Psalm 19:14

A quiet spirit is ....

Quiet

...but not always silent.

Psalm 39: 1-3; 19:14

I waited patiently for the Lord;

Psalm 40:1

If you should find yourself

Stuck in the mud...

call for rescue

<u>but</u>

be sure to ask directions for

The next step

your muddy feet should take!

Psalm 40:1-3; I John 5:14

GREAT PEACE

have they who love Your law...

nothing

can cause them to stumble.

Psalm 119:165

76

Be sure not to stumble
over the <u>very</u> elements
of God's will
Scattered along the course
He has set for you!

Psalm 119:165

... I have learned the secret
of being content....

Philippians 4:12

As long as my wants
do not exceed the limits
of my expectation,
I find myself quite content...
But when I reach beyond with no expectation
and find something more within my grasp,
it is indeed... a lovely thing!

Psalm 73:26; Philippians 4:12-13

...Never will I leave you,
never will I forsake you..

Hebrews 13:5

Elijah mistakenly thought he was alone
And the Lord opened His eyes to the many.

When I thought I was alone the Lord opened
my eyes to a few
And somehow
They felt like plenty!

Hebrews 13:5-6
1 Kings 19:1-18

... let us run with perseverance
the race marked out for us ...

Hebrews 12: 1

Sitting at a desk with much to do…
from a home where tasks never seem
complete…
encumbered with a weight of care…
even from the bed of those who suffer …
It is <u>always</u> <u>about the race</u>
The race never stops due to circumstances.
The race is always on!
Circumstances may alter the strategy
and the hindrances to be set aside…
But I need never forget that
Jesus ran the race and showed us how we
might run. The race is on and until the
race is over…
The prize awaits!

Hebrews 12:1-3; 10:35; 2 Timothy 4:7

Give thanks
in _all_ circumstances...

1 Thessalonians 5:18

GRATITUDE

May simply be

The highest "rung"

On a ladder,

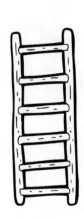

The foundation

Of which begins with

<u>appreciation</u>

I Thessalonians 5:18; Colossians 3:16

... I desire to do Your will, O My God...

Psalm 40:7-8

When weighed...
What is really of greater importance...

My hopes, dreams, and highest ambitions
Or
God's purpose and plans for me
and
how I live those out in a single day
over the course of my life?


Psalm 40:5, 7; Acts 13:36

...My grace is sufficient for you
... My power is made perfect
in weakness.


2 Corinthians 12:9

The promise of scripture is simple

THERE IS

sufficiency of God's grace

for every mountain and valley

and all the places in between

2 Corinthians 12:9

AND

nothing can THWART God's purposes!

Job 42:2

SO THAT

the Lord will fulfill His purpose for me...

Psalm 138:8a

As water reflects a face
... a man's heart reflects the man.
Proverbs 27:19

In spite of
what I know...   what I say...
what I teach...
It may take the most unexpected
Circumstances
to open my eyes and reveal
what I really believe ...
and to cleanse my heart!

2 Corinthians 4:4-5; Luke 16:15; Proverbs 27:19

Let us then approach the throne of grace
with confidence ...

Hebrews 4:16

In finding grace for the journey
in times of need,
I may discover asking for grace
for _just_ the next step
will sustain me for _all_ the miles ahead...

Lord, may I rely on your grace each step
of the way...

Hebrews 4:16; Lamentations 3:22-23

... my close friend
I have enjoyed sweet fellowship.

Psalm 55:13

Even if a "best friend"
is but for a season,
the friendship has
become a permanent,
if not significant
part of our own
Personal lifetime journey

Psalm 55:13; Proverbs 18:24

There is a time
for everything ...

Ecclesiastes 3: 1

Don't allow a friendship
to become
less than what it can be
BUT

never try to make it
more than what it should be!

Ecclesiastes 3:1, 5b

I will extol the LORD

at all times...


Psalm 34:1

Our Father,

Who art in heaven

hallowed be Thy name on earth

in

every thought I think

every word I speak

every step I take

and with

every beat of my

Psalm 34:1-3

Send forth
Your light and Your truth,
let them guide me...

Psalm 43:3

At the point ...

when the 💡 dawns,

and with clarity we see the actual reality

that surrounds us

then....

it is probably time to accept and move on

in light of what we now

know and see

to be true!

Psalm 43:3; 2 Kings 6:8-17

For the Lord is good and His love

endures forever;

His faithfulness ....

through all generations.


Psalm 100:5

In seasons of Wintery coolness and
gray skies
That seem will never end,
I need to remember the God ordained
Seasons yet to come...
The beautiful color of Spring bloom
The blue of Summer skies
The lovely hues of autumn.
But if this season of winter should last,
Then I would ask ...
You keep me close to the warmth of
Your heart

Genesis 8:22; Psalm 100:5

...yet I will rejoice....

Habakkuk 3:18

When your ♡
awakens
with a song of praise,
don't
allow the world
to change the tune...
Oh, yeah! ♫

Habakkuk 3:17-18

The secret things belong to God...

Deuteronomy 29:29

If

You

can

"figure out" a miracle....

then,

it's probably not one!

Romans 11:33-34: Deuteronomy 29:29

Let us

encourage one another....

Hebrews 10:25

Don't ignore the tiniest
seed of encouragement...

allow it to take root
in your heart
and grow!

Hebrews 10:25

It doesn't take a field of flowers
A simple bloom will do
Just call to mind <u>one blessing</u>
And let it carry you!
May you discover God's richest grace
And sweetest peace
As you recognize His "bouquet of blessings"
In your <u>own</u> life.

CPSIA information can be obtained
at www.ICGtesting.com
Printed in the USA
BVHW08s0026200918
527917BV00005B/17/P

9 781545 645185